Orton Gillingham Phonics Workbook

100 phonics activities for struggling readers and kids with dyslexia

VOLUME 3

BrainChild

Copyright 2022 - All Rights Reserved

Contents of this book may not be reproduced, duplicated or transmitted without direct written permission from the author. Under no circumstances will any legal responsibility or blame be held against the publisher for any reparation, damages or monetary loss due to information herein, either directly or indirectly

Legal Notice

You cannot amend, distribute, sell, use, quote or paraphrase any part of the contents within this book without the consent of the author.

Disclaimer Notice

Please note that the information contained within this document serves only for educational and entertainment purposes. No warranties of any kind are expressed or implied. Readers acknowledge that the author is not engaging in the rendering of legal, financial, medical or professional advice.

INTRODUCTION

Dyslexia is a learning disability that affects reading, writing, speaking and also the ability to do math or organize thoughts and ideas. This disorder affects the brain making it difficult to break words down into sounds, recognize them, and put them back together. Because of this, students have a hard time in school, that's why an early diagnosis is important so children may get the help they need. If left untreated, dyslexia can lead to:

- Low self-esteem
- Poor academic performance
- Poor future job prospects

Having access to specific activity books can help children with dyslexia learn to read while having fun.

INTRODUCTION

Find what you need about Phonetics in Orton Gillingham Phonics Workbook

Many children with dyslexia also have difficulties with oral language, speech, and nonverbal reasoning. Therefore, the most important thing you can do for them is to make sure they are not discouraged from reading or writing.

One of the best methods to assist them is with books that have activities focused specifically on phonetics to support them in learning sounds. For example, it is crucial to highlight the following aspects:

- Help them learn what words sound like when they are said out loud.
- Help them identify how letters look when they are written.

INTRODUCTION

Adding special activities focused on phonics encourages students to take ownership of their phonetic skills and develop an interest in reading early on. Students will learn how to breakdown words and how to correctly pronounce them when illustrated with images. This is how you can help reinforce their learning process.

What you will find in the book about Phonetics

This book was made for parents and students with the objective of providing early support during the learning process.

Summary of the activities found in the book

First, you will find exercises with beginning sounds. Here your child will see a box with two letters and a picture in the middle. What the child must do in this activity is to choose the first letter of the drawing that appears.

INTRODUCTION

For example, if it is a cake, they must select the letter "c". Then they must click on the picture to hear the sound.

The second exercise is quite like the first. However, here they must identify the final sound of the word. In this exercise, your child will see a picture and a word below; they must write the missing letter to complete it using the image as a help. Following are digraph exercises where students must read, trace letters and write words. These exercises are also complemented by drawings.

Lastly, you are going to see activities with short and long vowels. Here your child must write the missing letter to complete the words. Each one is accompanied by a drawing to make it easier for the child to identify and understand its meaning.

INTRODUCTION

Other advanced phonetic exercises in the book

Apart from the exercises that we have already explained, Phonics also includes a series of slightly more complex activities that students can do once they have finished the previous section. In addition, the number of exercises will allow them to practice and reinforce their knowledge. Here you will also find several CVC word exercises to help complete syllables with phonemes. Your child will have to choose the correct vowel to complete the word. Each one has a drawing so they can relate image, sound, and writing. Then they will find exercises with consonants; these activities are a bit like the exercises with vowels. However, here they must write the corresponding word in a box found below a drawing. The last exercise you will see is about consonant blending. These are the ones that, despite being together, keep their own sound. This is a slightly more dynamic activity in which the child must draw a line joining the drawing with the correct word.

INTRODUCTION

Special exercises about Phonetics

Although it is somewhat worrying, dyslexia is a disorder that can be treated early on. All the activities incorporated in this book have been specially designed and studied so that your child can learn to read and write while having fun!

TABLE OF CONTENTS

Phonics Sounds Letter A to Z 1-26
Beginning Sounds 27-44
Consonant Blends 45-54
CVC Words 55-66
Consonant Digraphs 67-72
Ending Sounds 73-84
R-Controlled Words 85-90
Short Vowels 91-95
Long Vowels 96-100

Aa

/aaa/

Directions: Trace and circle the picture that begins with the letter "A".

B b

/buh/

Directions: Trace and circle the picture that begins with the letter "B".

C c

/kuh/

Directions: Trace and circle the picture that begins with the letter "C".

3

Dd

/duh/

Directions: Trace and circle the picture that begins with the letter "D".

/eh/

Directions: Trace and circle the picture that begins with the letter "E".

F f

/fff/

Directions: Trace and circle the picture that begins with the letter "F".

Gg

/guh/

Directions: Trace and circle the picture that begins with the letter "G".

Hh

/huh/

Directions: Trace and circle the picture that begins with the letter "H".

Ii

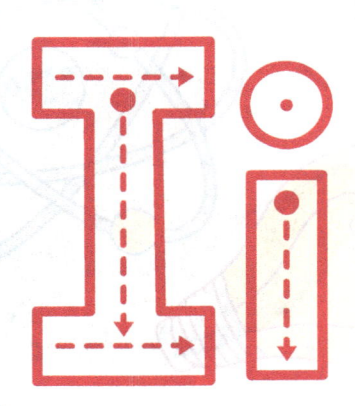

/iii/

Directions: Trace and circle the picture that begins with the letter "I".

Jj /juh/

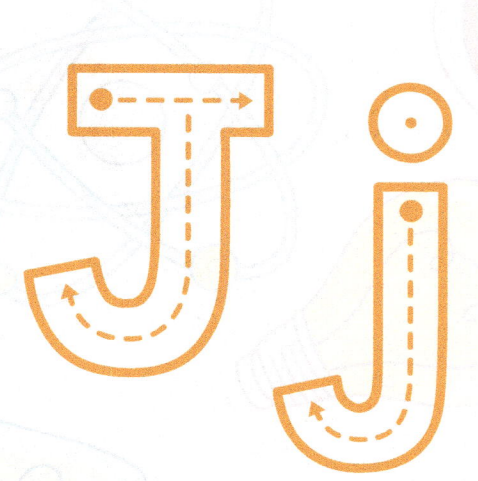

Directions: Trace and circle the picture that begins with the letter "J".

Kk

/kuh/

Directions: Trace and circle the picture that begins with the letter "K".

Ll

Directions: Trace and circle the picture that begins with the letter "L".

Mm /mmm/

Directions: Trace and circle the picture that begins with the letter "M".

Nn /nnn/

Directions: Trace and circle the picture that begins with the letter "N".

Directions: Trace and circle the picture that begins with the letter "O".

15

Pp

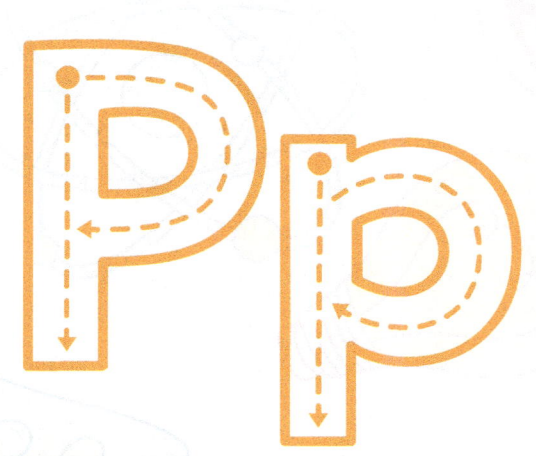

/puh/

Directions: Trace and circle the picture that begins with the letter "P".

16

Qq

/kwuh/

Directions: Trace and circle the picture that begins with the letter "Q".

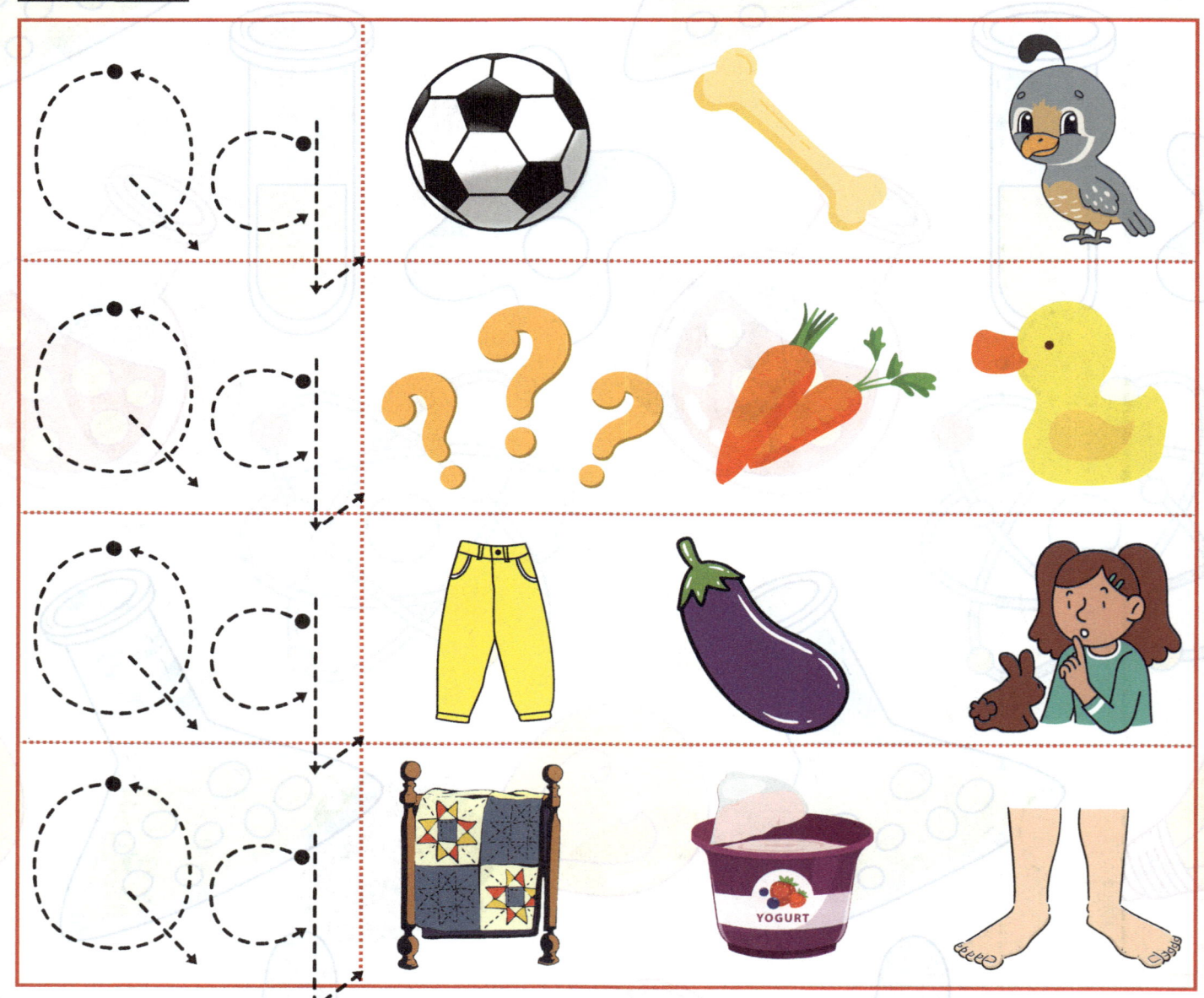

17

Rr

/rrr/

Directions: Trace and circle the picture that begins with the letter "R".

18

Ss

/sss/

Directions: Trace and circle the picture that begins with the letter "S".

19

T t

/tuh/

Directions: Trace and circle the picture that begins with the letter "T".

20

Uu

/uh/

Directions: Trace and circle the picture that begins with the letter "U".

Vv /vvv/

Directions: Trace and circle the picture that begins with the letter "V".

W w /wuh/

Directions: Trace and circle the picture that begins with the letter "W".

Xx

/kss/

Directions: Trace and circle the picture that begins with the letter "X".

24

/yyy/

Yy

Directions: Trace and circle the picture that begins with the letter "Y".

Zz

/zzz/

Directions: Trace and circle the picture that begins with the letter "Z".

BEGINNING SOUNDS

Directions: Match the pictures with the same beginning sounds.

BEGINNING SOUNDS

Directions: Match the pictures with the same beginning sounds.

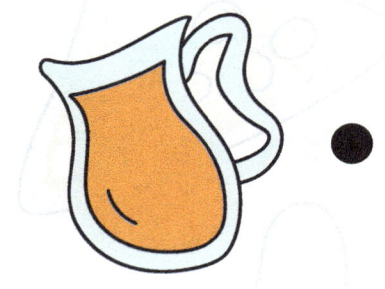

BEGINNING SOUNDS

Directions: Match the pictures with the same beginning sounds.

BEGINNING SOUNDS

Directions: Match the pictures with the same beginning sounds.

BEGINNING SOUNDS

Directions: Match the pictures with the same beginning sounds.

BEGINNING SOUNDS

Directions: Match the pictures with the same beginning sounds.

32

BEGINNING SOUNDS

Directions: Match the pictures with the same beginning sounds.

BEGINNING SOUNDS

Directions: Match the pictures with the same beginning sounds.

BEGINNING SOUNDS

Directions: Match the pictures with the same beginning sounds.

BEGINNING SOUNDS

Directions: Match the pictures with the same beginning sounds.

BEGINNING SOUNDS

Directions: Write the beginning letter of each picture in the box, then write the new produced word in the blank.

BEGINNING SOUNDS

Directions: Write the beginning letter of each picture in the box, then write the new produced word in the blank.

BEGINNING SOUNDS

Directions: Write the beginning letter of each picture in the box, then write the new produced word in the blank.

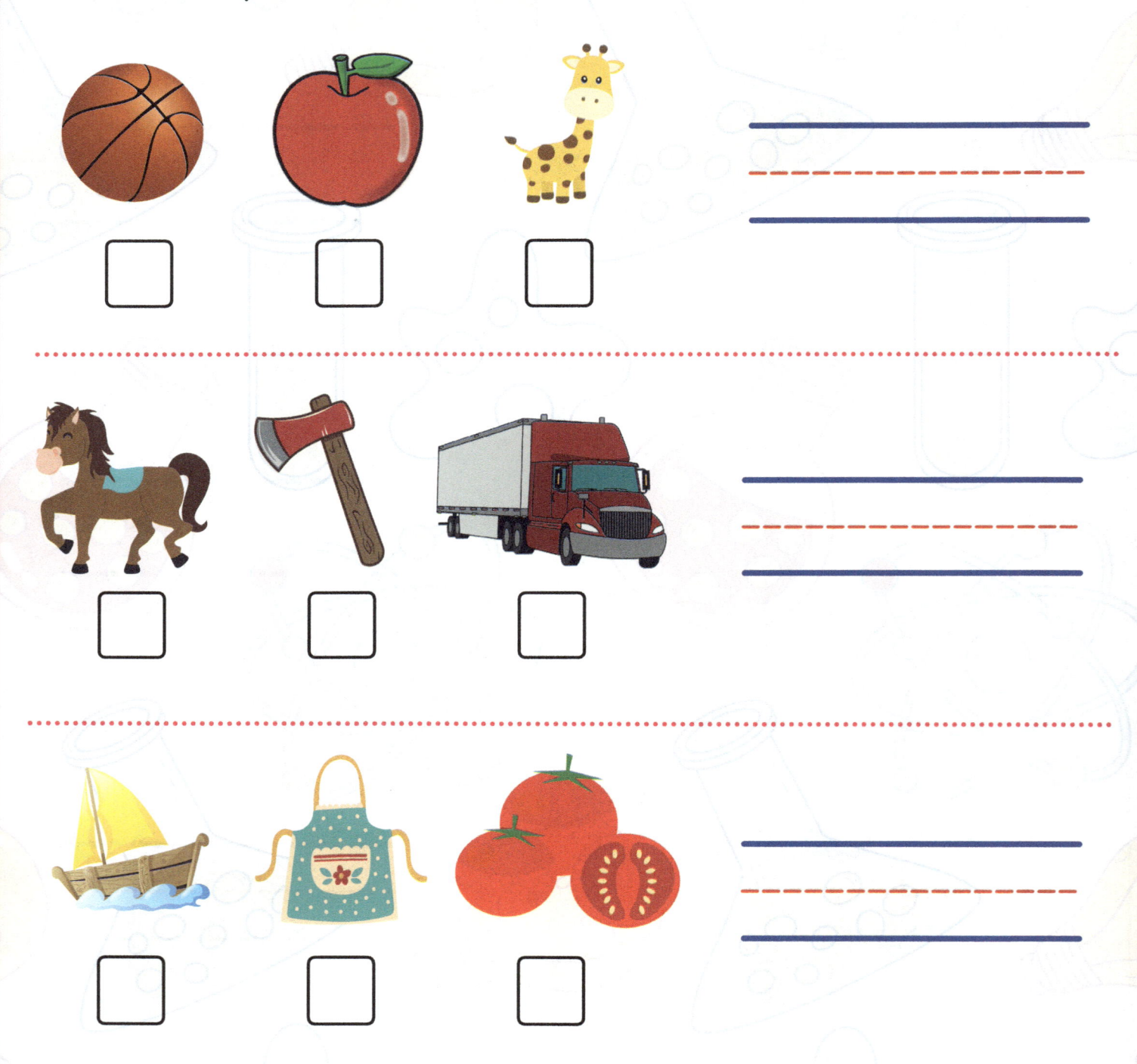

BEGINNING SOUNDS

Directions: Write the beginning letter of each picture in the box, then write the new produced word in the blank.

40

BEGINNING SOUNDS

Directions: Write the beginning letter of each picture in the box, then write the new produced word in the blank.

BEGINNING SOUNDS

Directions: Write the beginning letter of each picture in the box, then write the new produced word in the blank.

BEGINNING SOUNDS

Directions: Write the beginning letter of each picture in the box, then write the new produced word in the blank.

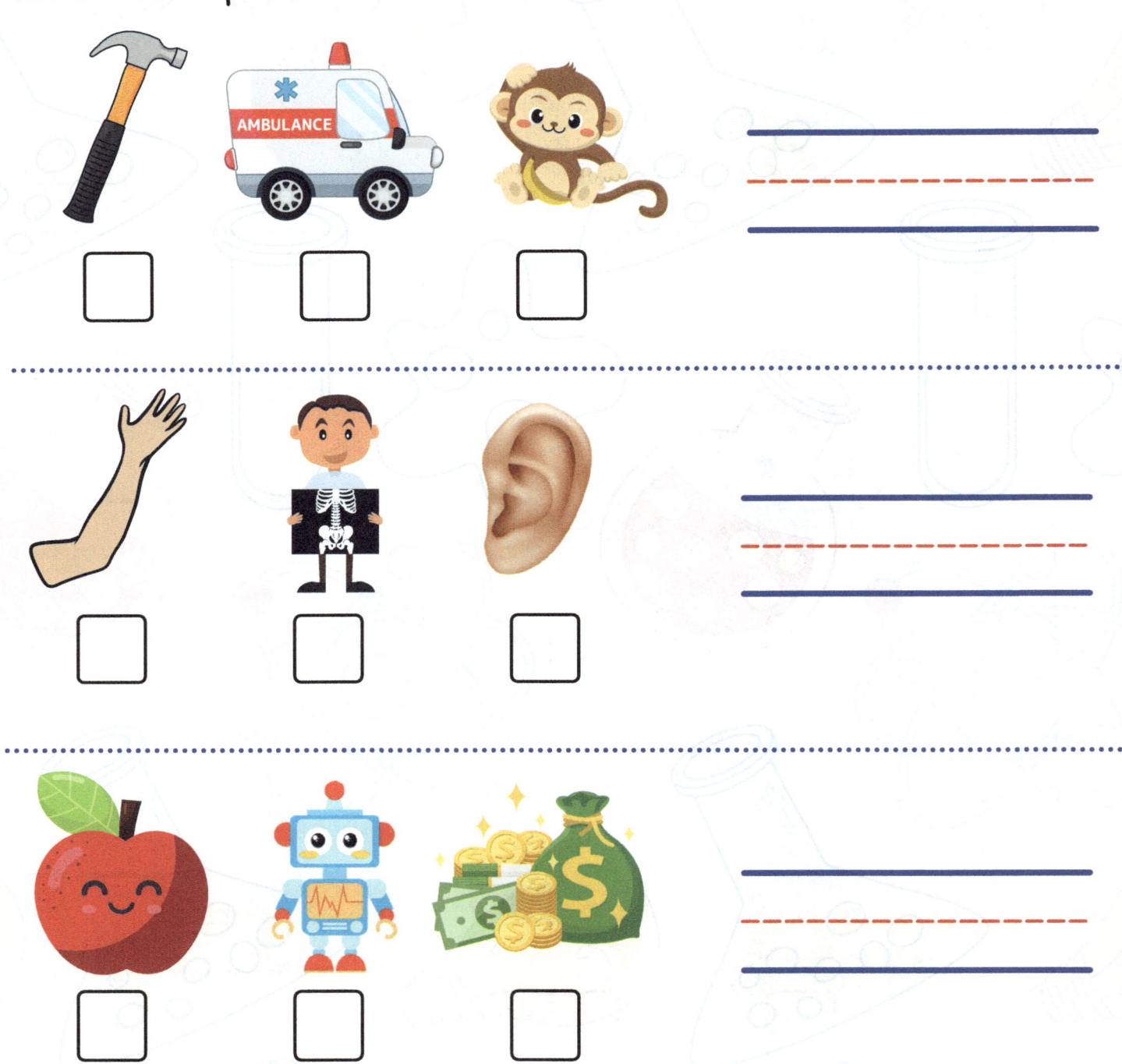

BEGINNING SOUNDS

Directions: Write the beginning letter of each picture in the box, then write the new produced word in the blank.

CONSONANT BLENDS

Directions: Fill in each blank with the correct consonant blend from the box.

| SN | TR | BR | GL | SW |
| FL | ST | DR | BL | |

__USH

__OCKS

__OVES

__UCK

__AR

__AMINGO

CONSONANT BLENDS

Directions: Fill in each blank with the correct consonant blend from the box.

| SN | TR | BR | GL | SW |
| FL | ST | DR | BL | |

__UM

__UMPET

__OBE

__OWER

__OW

__OMBONE

CONSONANT BLENDS

Directions: Fill in each blank with the correct consonant blend from the box.

SN	TR	BR	GL	SW
FL	ST	DR	BL	

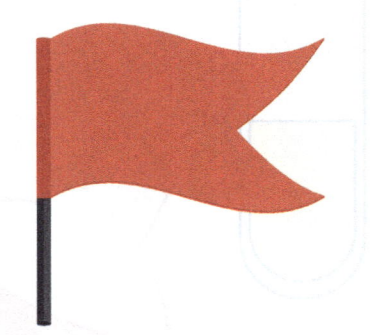

__AG

__ANKET

__AIL

__EE

__AN

__Y

CONSONANT BLENDS

Directions: Fill in each blank with the correct consonant blend from the box.

SN	CL	GR	GL	SL
SP	ST	DR	BL	

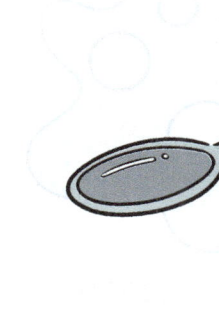

__ESS

__OON

__IDE

__OWN

__APES

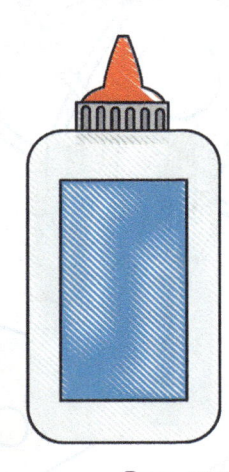

__UE

CONSONANT BLENDS

Directions: Fill in each blank with the correct consonant blend from the box.

| SL | TR | BR | GL | SW |
| FL | ST | CL | SC | |

__OTH

__IM

__OCK

__IDGE

__ALE

__OOM

CONSONANT BLENDS

Directions: Fill in each blank with the correct consonant blend from the box.

PL	TR	BR	GL	CR
SK	ST	DR	FR	

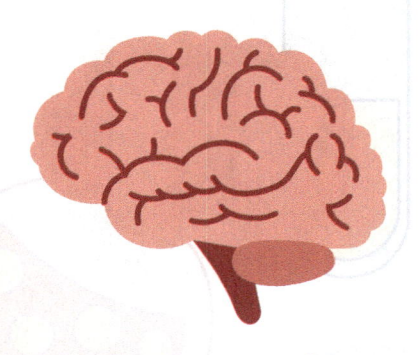

__AIN

__AB

__ANT

__ATE

__OOL

__OG

CONSONANT BLENDS

Directions: Fill in each blank with the correct consonant blend from the box.

PL	CR	BR	PR	SL
FL	ST	FR	BL	

__ED

__AYONS

__ETZEL

__UG

__ATUE

__UITS

CONSONANT BLENDS

Directions: Fill in each blank with the correct consonant blend from the box.

SN   SK   BR   GL   SW
SP   ST   DR   GR

__AGON

__ING

__ONGE

__ASS

__ASSES

__UNK

CONSONANT BLENDS

Directions: Fill in each blank with the correct consonant blend from the box.

SC	TR	BR	GL	SP
PL	SK	DR	CL	

__ARF

__IDER

__EAD

__I

__ANET

__OUD

CONSONANT BLENDS

Directions: Fill in each blank with the correct consonant blend from the box.

| CR | TR | BR | GL | SW |
| FL | ST | DR | BL | |

__OW

__ENDER

__OSS

__EASURE

__AIRS

__OWN

CVC WORDS

Directions: Write the missing letter for each CVC word. Write the word in the space provided.

| B | U | _ |

| B | _ | G |

| _ | O | X |

| B | O | _ |

CVC WORDS

Directions: Write the missing letter for each CVC word. Write the word in the space provided.

| L _ G | N _ T |

| _ I D | M O _ |

CVC WORDS

Directions: Write the missing letter for each CVC word. Write the word in the space provided.

Z _ P	_ A N

F I _	T _ B

CVC WORDS

Directions: Write the missing letter for each CVC word. Write the word in the space provided.

| W | E | _ |

| C | _ | T |

| _ | E | N |

| H | _ | T |

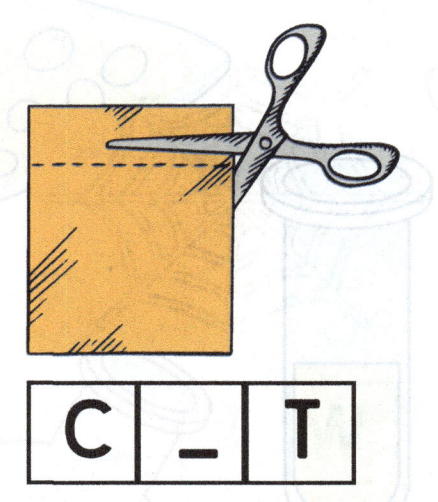

CVC WORDS

Directions: Write the missing letter for each CVC word. Write the word in the space provided.

| W | E | _ |

| B | _ | X |

| S | U | _ |

| T | O | _ |

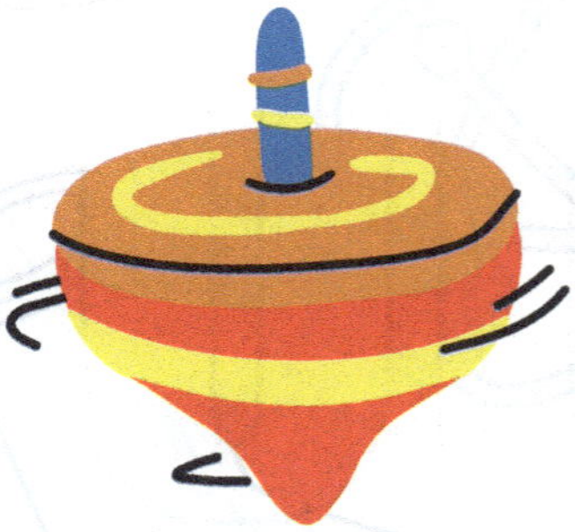

CVC WORDS

Directions: Write the missing letter for each CVC word. Write the word in the space provided.

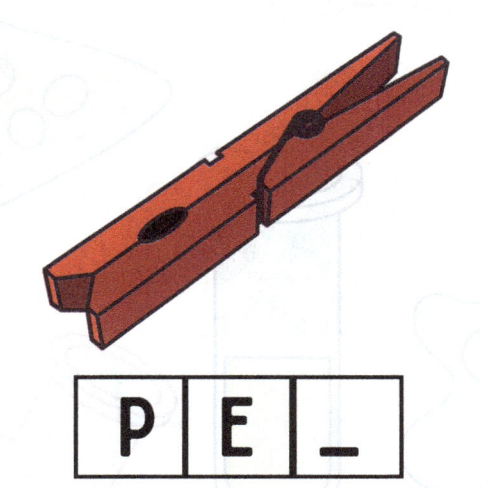

| P | E | _ |

| P | _ | N |

| _ | O | T |

| P | _ | G |

CVC WORDS

Directions: Write the missing letter for each CVC word. Write the word in the space provided.

D _ P	_ I G

J _ M	H _ M

CVC WORDS

Directions: Write the missing letter for each CVC word. Write the word in the space provided.

B _ D	B _ G

_ A N	R A _

CVC WORDS

Directions: Write the missing letter for each CVC word. Write the word in the space provided.

| C | A | _ |

| M | _ | P |

| _ | O | G |

| C | A | _ |

CVC WORDS

Directions: Write the missing letter for each CVC word. Write the word in the space provided.

| B | A | _ |

| J | E | _ |

| J | _ | G |

| N | U | _ |

64

CVC WORDS

Directions: Write the missing letter for each CVC word. Write the word in the space provided.

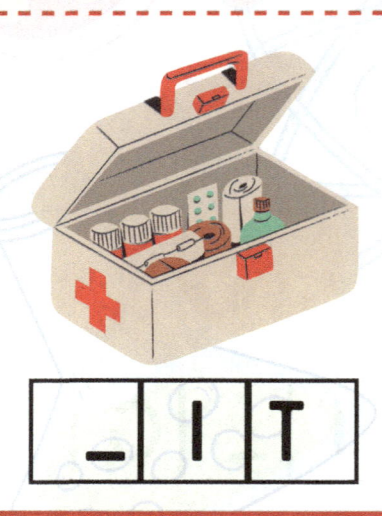

| V | A | _ |

| M | U | _ |

| P | O | _ |

| _ | I | T |

CVC WORDS

Directions: Write the missing letter for each CVC word. Write the word in the space provided.

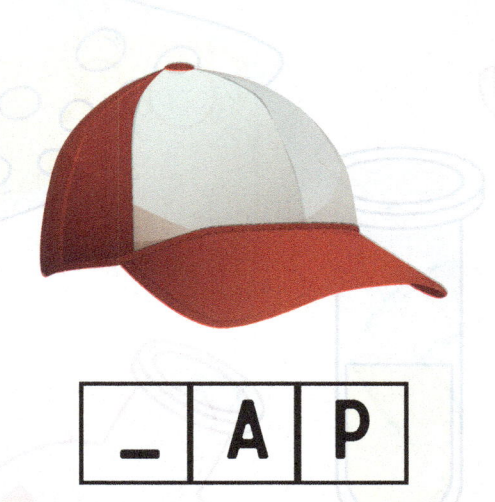

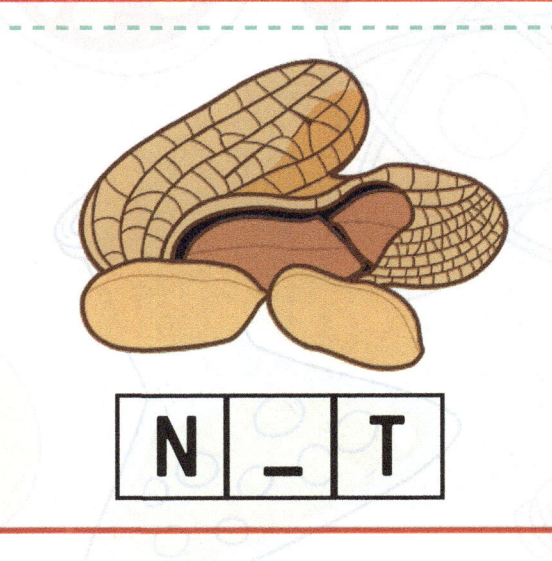

W _ G	_ A P

N _ P	N _ T

CONSONANT DIGRAPHS

Directions: Identify the digraph in each picture and shade the circle with the correct answer.

○ CK   ○ CH   ○ GH   ○ KN

○ CK   ○ CH   ○ GH   ○ KN

○ SH   ○ WH   ○ TH   ○ PH

○ CK   ○ CH   ○ GH   ○ KN

CONSONANT DIGRAPHS

Directions: Identify the digraph in each picture and shade the circle with the correct answer.

○ SH   ○ TH   ○ WH   ○ PH

○ CK   ○ CH   ○ GH   ○ KN

○ TH   ○ WH   ○ SH   ○ CH

○ CK   ○ CH   ○ GH   ○ KN

68

CONSONANT DIGRAPHS

Directions: Identify the digraph in each picture and shade the circle with the correct answer.

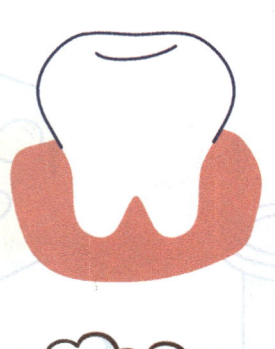

○ SH   ○ PH   ○ CH   ○ TH

○ SH   ○ PH   ○ CH   ○ TH

○ TH   ○ CH   ○ SH   ○ WH

○ WH   ○ TH   ○ PH   ○ SH

CONSONANT DIGRAPHS

Directions: Identify the digraph in each picture and shade the circle with the correct answer.

○ CH   ○ SH   ○ TH   ○ WH

○ CH   ○ SH   ○ TH   ○ WH

○ CH   ○ SH   ○ TH   ○ WH

○ CH   ○ SH   ○ TH   ○ WH

CONSONANT DIGRAPHS

Directions: Identify the digraph in each picture and shade the circle with the correct answer.

○ SH   ○ TH   ○ WH   ○ PH

○ SH   ○ TH   ○ PH   ○ WH

○ SH   ○ TH   ○ PH   ○ WH

○ SH   ○ TH   ○ WH   ○ PH

CONSONANT DIGRAPHS

Directions: Identify the digraph in each picture and shade the circle with the correct answer.

○ SH   ○ TH   ○ WH   ○ PH

○ SH   ○ TH   ○ CH   ○ PH

○ SH   ○ TH   ○ WH   ○ CH

○ SH   ○ TH   ○ PH   ○ WH

ENDING SOUNDS

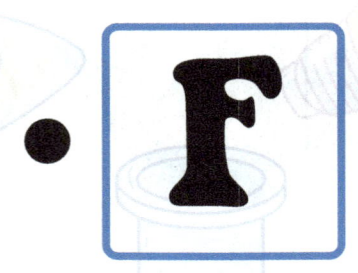

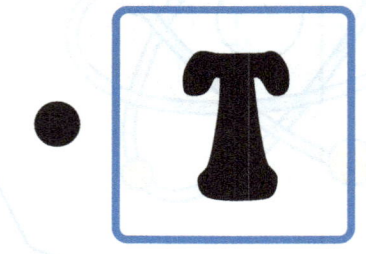

Directions: Match each picture to its ending sound.

F

E

T

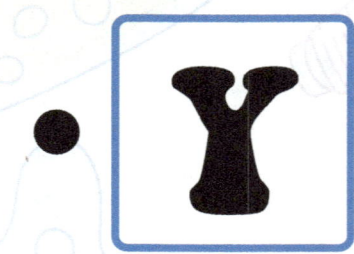

Y

ENDING SOUNDS

Directions: Match each picture to its ending sound.

74

ENDING SOUNDS

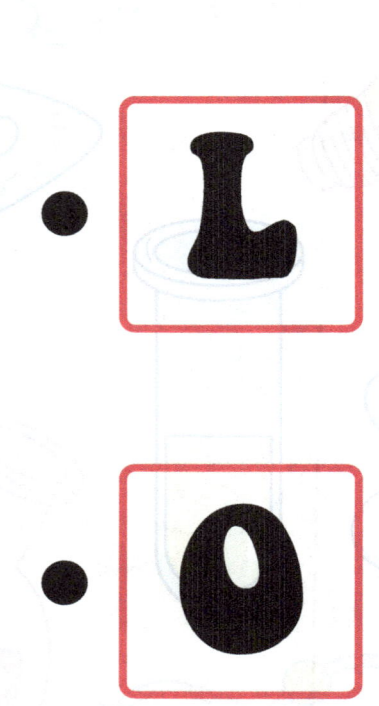

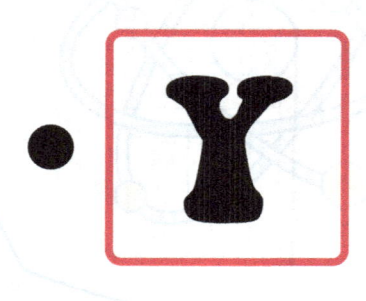

Directions: Match each picture to its ending sound.

🍅 tomato	L
☁️ snow	O
🐌 snail	Y
🪰 fly	W

75

ENDING SOUNDS

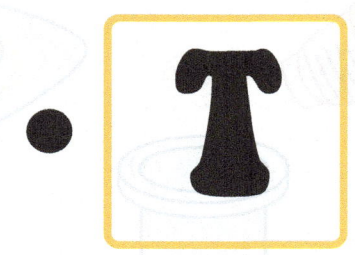

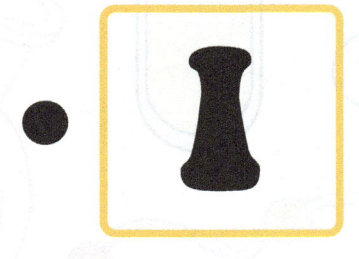

Directions: Match each picture to its ending sound.

- T
- I
- N
- R

ENDING SOUNDS

Directions: Match each picture to its ending sound.

D

R

F

G

77

ENDING SOUNDS

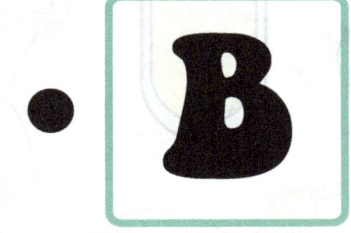

Directions: Match each picture to its ending sound.

- broccoli •   • D
- bee •   • B
- crab •   • E
- gold bars •   • I

ENDING SOUNDS

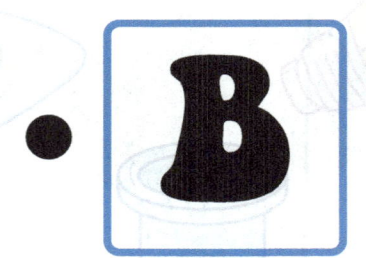

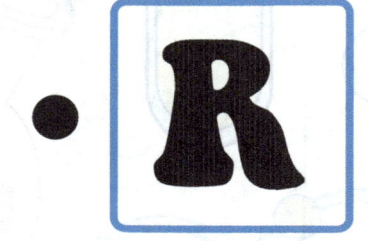

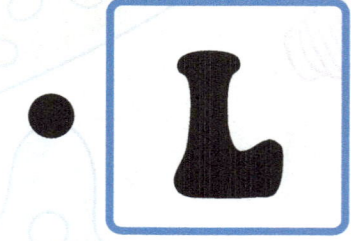

Directions: Match each picture to its ending sound.

- grasshopper •   • B
- bell •   • R
- lightbulb •   • P
- lamp •   • L

ENDING SOUNDS

Directions: Match each picture to its ending sound.

T

K

O

Y

ENDING SOUNDS

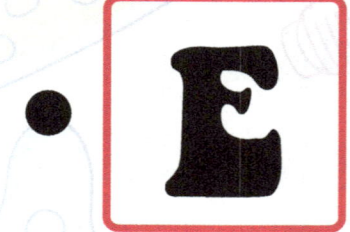

Directions: Match each picture to its ending sound.

P

S

Y

E

ENDING SOUNDS

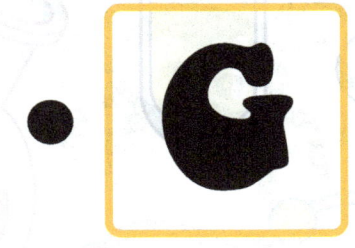

Directions: Match each picture to its ending sound.

- 🐶 •   • R
- 🐘 •   • G
- 🐴 •   • T
- 🐓 •   • E

ENDING SOUNDS

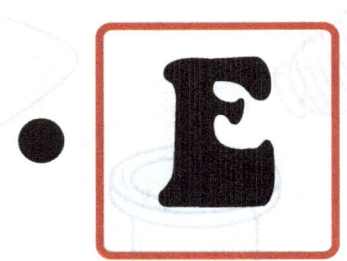

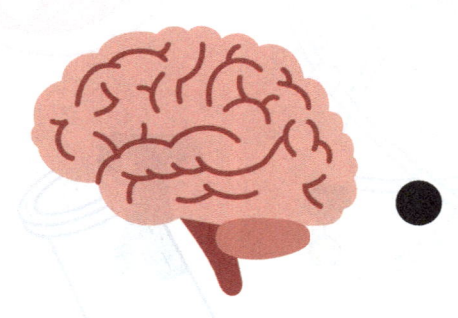

Directions: Match each picture to its ending sound.

- cow •   • E
- spider •   • W
- brain •   • R
- slide •   • N

ENDING SOUNDS

Directions: Match each picture to its ending sound.

- F
- R
- T
- N

R- CONTROLLED WORDS

DIRECTIONS: COLOR THE EASTER EGGS WITH R-CONTROLLED VOWELS USING THE COLOR KEY TO MARK "UR", "AR", "ER", "OR", AND "IR" DISTINCTLY.

ER = ORANGE
AR = RED
OR = BLUE
UR = GREEN
IR = VIOLET

- BURN
- HARD
- CLERK
- GIRL
- BARN
- ARM
- TURN
- DOOR
- CURL

R- CONTROLLED WORDS

DIRECTIONS: COLOR THE EASTER EGGS WITH R-CONTROLLED VOWELS USING THE COLOR KEY TO MARK "UR", "AR", "ER", "OR", AND "IR" DISTINCTLY.

ER = ORANGE
AR = RED
OR = BLUE
UR = GREEN
IR = VIOLET

- DIRT
- ART
- CURL
- NORTH
- STIR
- MARK
- BEER
- BAR
- CAR

86

R- CONTROLLED WORDS

DIRECTIONS: COLOR THE EASTER EGGS WITH R-CONTROLLED VOWELS USING THE COLOR KEY TO MARK "UR", "AR", "ER", "OR", AND "IR" DISTINCTLY.

ER = ORANGE
AR = RED
OR = BLUE
UR = GREEN
IR = VIOLET

- DEER
- FARM
- STORM
- START
- TURTLE
- DART
- BIRD
- TIGER
- SHARK

R- CONTROLLED WORDS

DIRECTIONS: COLOR THE EASTER EGGS WITH R-CONTROLLED VOWELS USING THE COLOR KEY TO MARK "UR", "AR", "ER", "OR", AND "IR" DISTINCTLY.

ER= ORANGE
AR= RED
OR= BLUE
UR= GREEN
IR= VIOLET

- CIRCLE
- PURSE
- BIRTH
- CARD
- FORK
- PORK
- HURT
- GERM
- WORM

R- CONTROLLED WORDS

DIRECTIONS: COLOR THE EASTER EGGS WITH R-CONTROLLED VOWELS USING THE COLOR KEY TO MARK "UR", "AR", "ER", "OR", AND "IR" DISTINCTLY.

ER= ORANGE
AR= RED
OR= BLUE
UR= GREEN
IR= VIOLET

- HER
- PARK
- CAR
- PART
- HORN
- SHARP
- FAR
- CHURCH
- FUR

R- CONTROLLED WORDS

DIRECTIONS: COLOR THE EASTER EGGS WITH R-CONTROLLED VOWELS USING THE COLOR KEY TO MARK "UR", "AR", "ER", "OR", AND "IR" DISTINCTLY.

- ER = ORANGE
- AR = RED
- OR = BLUE
- UR = GREEN
- IR = VIOLET

- YARD
- SHORT
- BARK
- COLOR
- HERB
- SHARP
- FIRST
- CHARM
- THIRD

SHORT VOWELS

Directions: Color the jar with the short "A" sound in each pair and write the word in the box.

PAD   PAID   LAND   LAID

BAKE   BAR   RAN   RAIN

SHORT VOWELS

Directions: Color the jar with the short "E" sound in each pair and write the word in the box.

NET NAPE

BED BEAD

WAIT WEB

HEN HEY

SHORT VOWELS

Directions: Color the jar with the short "I" sound in each pair and write the word in the box.

MEAT   MILK

KEEP   ZIP

TIN   TEEN

GEAR   GIFT

SHORT VOWELS

Directions: Color the jar with the short "O" sound in each pair and write the word in the box.

| HOSE | DOLL | | DOG | SOAP |

| POT | PAW | | HOST | SOCK |

SHORT VOWELS

Directions: Color the jar with the short "U" sound in each pair and write the word in the box.

BUG   BAG   MUG   MAP

SON   SUN   RUN   RAN

LONG VOWELS

Directions: Color the jar with the long "A" sound in each pair and write the word in the box.

| SAD | SAY | | BAKE | BACK |

| GLAD | GAIN | | TRAP | TAPE |

LONG VOWELS

Directions: Color the jar with the long "E" sound in each pair and write the word in the box.

BEAR	BEER

TEA	TIN

SLEEP	SLIP

BEE	BIN

LONG VOWELS

Directions: Color the jar with the long "I" sound in each pair and write the word in the box.

KIT   KITE   NIGHT   KNIT

PINE   PIN   DICE   DIM

LONG VOWELS

Directions: Color the jar with the long "O" sound in each pair and write the word in the box.

| HOME | HOT | | BOW | BUT |

| GONE | GOLD | | HOW | HOE |

LONG VOWELS

Directions: Color the jar with the long "U" sound in each pair and write the word in the box.

| MOON | MUD | | SOUP | SUN |

| GUN | GLUE | | DUCK | BLUE |

Other Brainchild Books Available on amazon

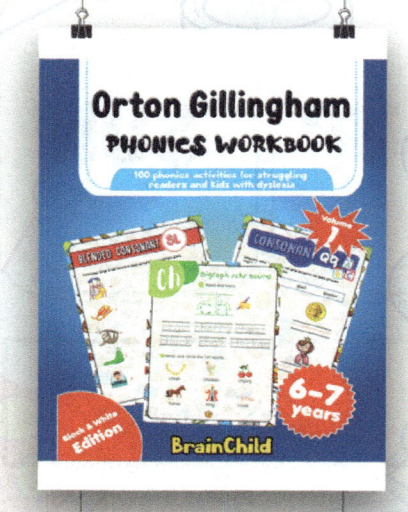

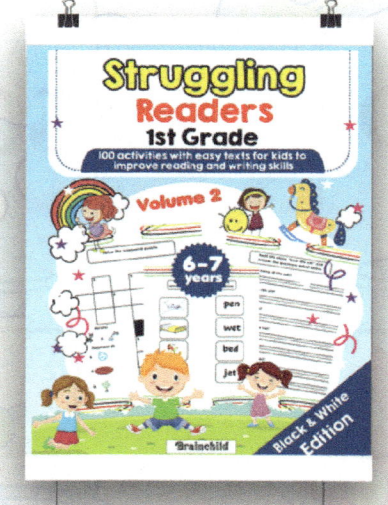

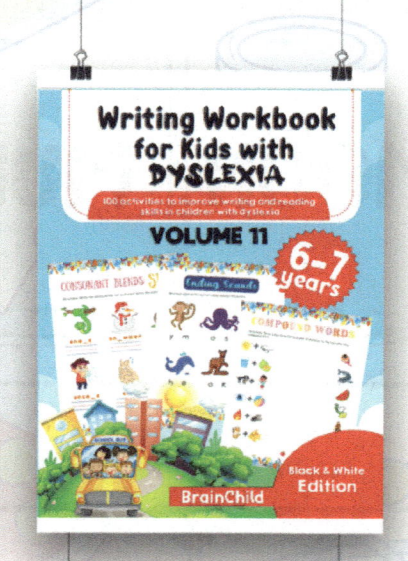

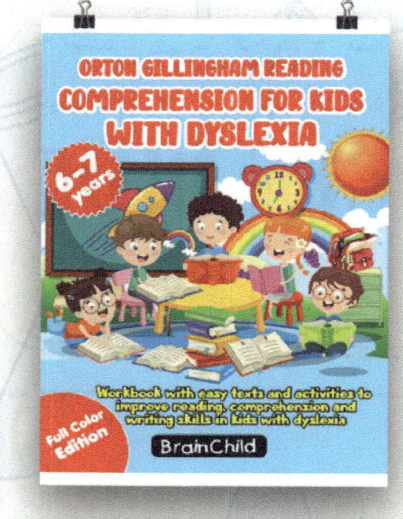

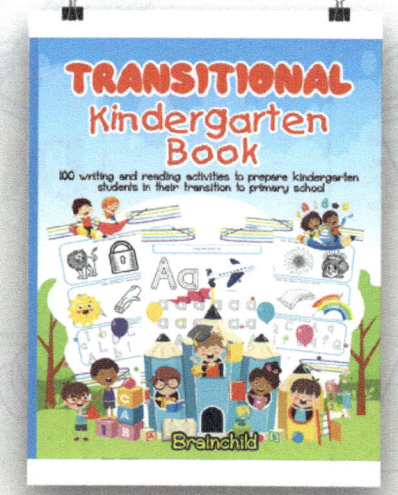

Made in the USA
Las Vegas, NV
14 February 2025